"Ew, David!"
and other quotes

Published by OH!
20 Mortimer Street
London W1T 3JW

Compilation text © 2021 Welbeck Non-Fiction Limited
Design © 2021 Welbeck Non-Fiction Limited

ISBN 978-1-80069-069-1

Compiled by: Katie Meegan   Editorial: Victoria Godden
Project manager: Russell Porter   Design: Andy Jones
Production: Freencky Portas

A CIP catalogue for this book is available from the Library of Congress

Printed in Dubai

10 9 8 7 6 5 4 3 2 1

"Ew, David!"
and other quotes

THE LITTLE GUIDE TO
SCHITT'S CREEK

CONTENTS

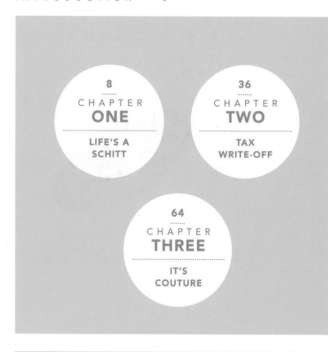

INTRODUCTION

For six glorious seasons, *Schitt's Creek* has delighted viewers all over the world. Written by father–son duo Eugene and Dan Levy, one could have never guessed at the sitcom's international acclaim from its humble beginnings on Canadian television. The show quickly became a fan favourite, gathering followers through word of mouth and the occasional viral Moira meme. Soon, *Schitt's Creek* was picked up by Netflix, and the small town with a big heart was launched on the international stage, drawing admirers from the USA to Japan, England to India.

When their fortune is squandered by a corrupt accountant, the once A-list Rose family find themselves left with nothing, apart from the deed to a town they once bought as a joke. They are greeted by the eclectic townspeople from unconventional major Roland Schitt, sarcastic Stevie and sunny Twyla. It's a far cry from a mansion to a motel, and the Rose family struggle to get on their designer-clad feet, finding friendship, love and many a mishap along the way.

The brainchild of Dan Levy, the idea for the series came to him when he wondered what a super-rich family, like the Kardashians, would do if they lost all their money. The resulting sitcom was not only one of Netflix's most streamed shows of 2020, but it also broke records at the Emmys, claiming an unprecedented nine awards across all the major comedy categories. The series ended on its 80th episode in 2020, but the inhabitants of Schitt's Creek will be in the hearts of audiences for many, many years to come.

So now is your chance to become a part of the Rose family, as we follow the cast through their words of wisdom and wisecracks on everything from bad days to bébés, food to fashion, careers to celebrities, and from family to forever love.

Best wishes, warmest regards.

CHAPTER
ONE

LIFE'S A SCHITT

QUOTES FOR A BAD DAY

You know those days when life is a bit, well, Schitt? The Rose family have been there. Whether it's a bad day at the office, fighting with your roommate/sibling or losing your vast fortune, we have a quote to get you through.

The world is falling apart around us, and I'm dying inside.

Moira Rose *expresses that feeling we've all had on a bad day.*

As seen on *screenrant.com, March 21, 2020, by Amanda Steele*

"

I plan on popping a pill, crying a bit, and falling asleep early.

"

David on his rather lacklustre birthday plans.

As seen on scarymommy.com, January 14, 2021, by Laura Grainger

This is a real *Sophie's Choice.*

Roland *gives us a rare insight into his decision-making process.*

As seen on *elitedaily.com, January 6, 2021,*
by Rachel Chapman

"

I'm trying very hard not to connect with people right now.

"

David *on his fragile emotional state.*

As seen on *scarymommy.com, January 14, 2021,*
by Laura Grainger

Oh, I'd kill for a good coma right now!

Moira *applying her soap opera training to grim reality.*

As seen on *screenrant.com, March 21, 2020, by Amanda Steele*

66

I'm only doing this because you called me rude, and I take that as a compliment.

99

Stevie *has a rather unusual approach to customer service at the Rosebud Motel.*

As seen on scarymommy.com, January 14, 2021, by Laura Grainger

It's just one long string of really bad luck and I don't know what kind of carnage I inflicted in my past life to deserve it. I must have been Dracula or a spin instructor or something.

David bemoans the ill fortune that seems to consistently befall his family.

As seen on *readersdigest.ca, September 18, 2020,* by Brett Walther

66

You are blind to reality and
for that I am most proud.

99

***Moira** encourages David to follow
her rules of engagement, or rather
disengagement, for life.*

As seen on *screenrant.com, March 21, 2020,
by Amanda Steele*

I'm incapable of faking sincerity.

Stevie *getting honest,*
or sarcastic, or both.

As seen on *scarymommy.com, January 14, 2021,*
by Laura Grainger

66

David, stop acting like a disgruntled pelican.

99

Moira asks David to be polite in her unique manner.

As seen on *screenrant.com*, March 21, 2020, by Amanda Steele

You know, being approachable isn't that important anyway, The Queen hasn't smiled since the '70s, and her birthdays are still very well attended.

David *on why being friendly and approachable is overrated.*

As seen on *scarymommy.com, January 14, 2021, by Laura Grainger*

THE FACTS

Dan Levy wears many hats – as well as playing David, he is the show's writer and showrunner. But did you know that his first job was on the reality television show *The Hills*? He hosted the aftershow, which inspired his ability to create the brilliantly eccentric Rose family. Speaking to *The Guardian*, he admitted that working behind the scenes turned him off that genre of television. "I think that when you work in reality TV, it kind of pulls back the curtain in a way that doesn't necessarily make you want to watch more of it." Thank God he turned to sitcoms!

> **"**
> Who knows what will befall us tomorrow, John? You could be hit by a Mack truck or bopped on the head by a tiny piece of space debris. **"**

Moira on the fickle nature of life.

As seen on *scarymommy.com, December 22, 2020,*
by Laura Grainger

66

I miss being surrounded by loose acquaintances who think I'm funny and smart and charming.

99

Alexis bemoans her former
life of partying and admirers.

As seen on eonline.com, April 7, 2020,
by Lauren Piester, Chris Harnick

Let's go. I've had enough waking hours for one day.

Moira's approach to time-management is very on-brand.

As seen on *everdaypower.com, November 9, 2020,* by Nia Simone McLeod

66

Talk to the hand, son, because the ears are no longer working.

99

Johnny gets down with the kids with the cool lingo.

As seen on *yourtango.com*, October 30, 2020, by Jaycee Levin

> **"**
>
> How mercurial is life … we all imagine being carried from the ashes by the goddess Artemis and here I get a balatron from Barnum & Bailey. **"**

***Moira** suffering at the uncaring hands of fate, or in other words, experiencing a minor inconvenience.*

As seen on *scarymommy.com, December 22, 2020, by Laura Grainger*

66

David: Okay, nobody freaked out when Alexis went missing.

Alexis: I didn't go missing, David. The FBI knew where I was the entire time.

99

The Rose siblings compare the differences between their disappearances.

As seen on *TVQuot.es, January 16, 2021*

I have never heard someone say so many wrong things, one after the other, consecutively, in a row.

__David__ tells Moira to curb her assumptions on Alexis's love life.

As seen on *elitedaily.com, November 2, 2020, by Rachel Chapman*

66

Let's all go to bed and pray we don't wake up.

99

Moira *ending a hard day on a rather…*
positive note.

As seen on scarymommy.com, December 22, 2020,
by Laura Grainger

I don't skate through life, David.
I walk through life, in really
nice shoes.

Alexis *on her life's motto.*

As seen on yourtango.com, October 30, 2020,
by Jaycee Levin

THE FACTS

When Johnny Rose buys David a town as a joke, it sets off the chain reaction of the newly broke family settling in Schitt's Creek. However, did you know that a super-rich Hollywood star buying a town is actually based on a true story? In 1989, Kim Basinger, of *James Bond* and *Batman* fame, bought the town of Brasleton, Georgia for a whopping $20 million dollars. At the time, the town had a population of just 500 and Basinger had plans to turn the town into a theme park or film studio. Alas, her plans went awry and she started selling off parts of the town during the 1990s.

I've been gutted. I've been stripped of every morsel of pleasure I've earned in this life.

Moira *on her riches-to-rags downfall.*

As seen on scarymommy.com, December 22, 2020, by Laura Grainger

66

I'm gonna pass. I'm not really in
the mood to be a victim of a hate
crime tonight.

99

David turns down Stevie's invite to
a party with the Schitt's Creek locals.

As seen on *mamasgeeky.com. January 7, 2020,
by Mama's Geeky*

Never let the bastards
get you down!

Moira has a Dead Poets Society *moment*
while teaching high school drama.

As seen on *scarymommy.com, December 22, 2020,*
by Laura Grainger

66

I am suddenly overwhelmed with regret. It's a new feeling for me, and I don't find it at all pleasurable.

99

Moira *suddenly encounters a new emotion after the leaking of her nudes.*

As seen on *readersdigest.ca*, September 18, 2020, by Brett Walther

CHAPTER
TWO

TAX
WRITE-OFF

ON CAREERS
AND MONEY

It's a tax write-off! Following their misfortune, the Rose family need to work, some of them for the first time. Whether it's selecting local merchandise for Rose Apothecary, starting your own PR firm, or running America's second-largest chain of video stores, let these quotes inspire your career.

66

You do realize I'm a professional vocalist?

99

Moira *makes a pitch for leader of the Jazzagals.*

As seen on scarymommy.com, December 22, 2020, by Laura Grainger

66

If you're looking for an ass to kiss, it's mine.

99

Roland introduces himself in his typical mayoral fashion.

As seen on *elitedaily.com, January 6, 2020, by Rachel Chapman*

"
Oh, I know I don't have any
money, but I need to *look* like
I don't have money. **"**

Johnny on his tactics for getting the
best deal on a second-hand car.

As seen on *readersdigest.ca, September 18, 2020,*
by Brett Walther

"
The idea of me life coaching another human being should scare you...a lot.

"

David reconsiders his career options in light of his new circumstances.

As seen on *elitedaily.com, November 2, 2020,* by Rachel Chapman

> 66
>
> The North Korean army could not keep my mother under control when it comes to event planning.
>
> 99

David warns all who might cross Moira on her event-planning warpath.

As seen on mamasgeeky.com, January 7, 2020, by Mama's Geeky

TAX WRITE-OFF

"

It's just a checkpoint, okay?
I've been through tons of these
in Johannesburg. Umm, it's
like a drive thru, except
everybody has a gun.

"

Alexis has some experience in moving a certain type of "merchandise".

As seen on readersdigest.ca, September 18, 2020, by Brett Walther

I'm not seeing anything in trend forecasting or art curating. That's weird.

Stevie *tempers David's job-seeking ambitions.*

As seen on *mamasgeeky.com, January 7, 2020,*
by Mama's Geeky

66

I'm positively bedeviled
with meetings et cetera.

99

Moira's *schedule is too full*
to help around the motel.

As seen on *scarymommy.com, December 22, 2020,*
by Laura Grainger

Tweet us on Facebook!

Johnny Rose *gets to grips*
with social media.

As seen on *yourtango.com, October 30, 2020,*
by Jaycee Levin

THE FACTS

Feeling stuck in your career?
Why not create your own opportunities,
like Dan Levy? After hosting on MTV
Canada for six years, Levy found it
difficult to land acting jobs as his anxiety
made him "terrible at auditioning".
Sick of rejection, he started writing and
eventually he had the idea for *Schitt's
Creek*. And the rest, as they say, is history!

Patrick: We just need a body.
David: Then go to the morgue.

David and Patrick *discuss the possibility of hiring for Rose Apothecary.*

As seen on *scarymommy.com, January 14, 2021, by Laura Grainger*

66

And who's to say what we can pull off? I recently heard of a small town in Scotland—no bigger than a thimble—that is making millions from a week-long singles fest. Now, if an idea as simple as that can work for a people as infamously disorganized as the Scotch, surely we can aspire to something of equal scale.

99

Moira gives a rousing speech to the volunteers at the Schitt's Creek first annual Singles' Week.

As seen on readersdigest.ca, September 18, 2020,
by Brett Walther

I can hardly hear you, John!
The cheering and accolades are
drowning out your gentle voice.

Moira glowing in the praise of
her triumph in local politics.

As seen on scarymommy.com, December 22, 2020,
by Laura Grainger

66

If those bunnies feel exploited even a little bit, I am pulling the plug.

99

Ted raises his concerns over
Alexis's bunny cam.

As seen on *scarymommy.com, January 14, 2021,*
by Laura Grainger

If there is anyone at this fabulous little confab who knows how to work a room of fragile egos, it's me. I once hosted the non-televised portion of the People's Choice Awards.

__Moira__ showcases her credentials which make her qualified for, errr, motel work.

As seen on everdaypower.com, November 9, 2020, by Nia Simone McLeod

"

Don't take this the wrong way, but is this car your home?

"

__Moira__ struggles to relate to her new neighbours, and Roland in particular.

As seen on *readersdigest.ca, September 18, 2020,*
by Brett Walther

Hashtag. Is that two words?

Johnny's social media brand awareness strategy seems to be going well.

As seen on *yourtango.com, October 30, 2020,* by Jaycee Levin

"

You are bored, lethargic, and practically dripping with ennui.

"

Moira encourages David to go back to work.

As seen on *scarymommy.com, December 22, 2020, by Laura Grainger*

THE FACTS

Eugene Levy originally didn't want Annie Murphy to play Alexis. Speaking to *Vulture*, Murphy recalled: "I was a brunette when I auditioned. And Eugene was having a really, really hard time wrapping his head around the fact that Alexis is blonde and Annie Murphy is brunette. He couldn't quite get there, so Dan had to tape pictures of blonde hair on my picture." It's hard to imagine anyone else as a little bit Alexis!

"

Children, keep an eye on these bags. Apparently in hell, there's no bellman!

"

Moira adjusts to the family's
new living arrangements.

As seen on *readersdigest.ca*, September 18, 2020,
by Brett Walther

Just remember: no sudden movements, do not reach for the glove box, and no matter what happens, do not tell them your real name.

Alexis *possesses a worrying amount of knowledge about smuggling items through police checkpoints.*

As seen on *scarymommy.com, January 14, 2021,* by Laura Grainger

"

Well, if I find out that you're accusing me of doing something I didn't do, then I'm going to accuse you of making false accusations.

"

*All's fair in love and politics, according to **Roland Schitt.***

As seen on *elitedaily.com, January 6, 2020, by Rachel Chapman*

I manned that front desk
with the vigour of a wartime
radio operator.

Moira on her brief stint at
the motel reception.

As seen on *everdaypower.com, November 9, 2020,
by Nia Simone McLeod*

66

Johnny: [reading] I was served by an intimidating woman at the front desk, with an unrecognizable accent, and scary-looking attire.

Moira: And what might this have to do with me?

99

Johnny deals with a negative review from a challenging motel guest, and an even more challenging wife.

As seen on *scarymommy.com, December 22, 2020, by Laura Grainger*

CHAPTER
THREE

IT'S COUTURE

STYLE AND SWEATERS

Even in their darkest hour, the Rose family still bring their classy, if eccentric, sense of style with them. From Moira's many wigs, to David's never-ending supply of black sweaters, what the family wears speaks volumes, darlings.

66

Is there like, a Texas Chainsaw movie being filmed out there that I'm not aware of?

99

David is taken aback by Roland's style, or lack thereof.

As seen on scarymommy.com, January 14, 2021, by Laura Grainger

66

My great-grandmother took it from her husband when she left him and it has been passed down through all the women in my family as emergency currency in case we need to leave our husbands in the middle of the night.

99

Moira explains the importance of her vintage brown bag.

As seen on *readersdigest.ca, September 18, 2020,* by Brett Walther

Allow me to offer you some advice. Take a thousand naked pictures of yourself now. You may currently think, 'Oh, I'm too spooky,' or 'Nobody wants to see these tiny boobies,' but believe me: one day you will look at those photos with much kinder eyes and say, 'Dear God, I was a beautiful thing!'

***Moira** gives Stevie some surprisingly body-positive advice.*

As seen on *scarymommy.com, January 14, 2021, by Laura Grainger*

66

Like Beyoncé, I excel as a solo artist and my mom dressed me well into my teens.

99

David feels a kinship with Queen B
on multiple levels.

As seen on *readersdigest.ca, September 18, 2020,*
by Brett Walther

You might want to rethink the nightgown first. There's a whole Ebenezer Scrooge thing happening. My best to Bob Cratchet.

David questions Johnny's choice of Christmas Eve attire.

As seen on *eonline.com*, April 7, 2020, by Lauren Piester, Chris Harnick

66

Stevie: My car is worth less than your pants.
David: Well, I've seen your car and that makes sense to me.

99

Stevie and David *discuss the practicality of their respective purchases.*

As seen on *scarymommy.com, January 14, 2021, by Laura Grainger*

If you ever see me shopping at Blouse Barn, you must shoot me in the temple.

Moira pleads with her family to not let her morph into the local style.

As seen on mamasgeeky.com, January 7, 2020, by Mama's Geeky

"

I haven't bedazzled anything
since I was twenty-two.

"

David's *style seems to have*
evolved with age.

As seen on eonline.com, April 7, 2020,
by Lauren Piester, Chris Harnick

"

Funky is a neon t-shirt you buy at an airport gift shop next to a bejewelled iPhone case. This is luxury.

"

__David__ takes offense to Stevie's description of his expansive wardrobe.

As seen on *scarymommy.com, January 14, 2021, by Laura Grainger*

THE FACTS

All of the designer clothes worn on the show are second-hand. Dan Levy felt that it was important for the Rose family to wear real designer clothing, but in the initial seasons they were on a tight budget. The costume designer often shopped in thrift stores, limited to a spend of no more than $200 per item.

David: I got these at a showroom in Paris.
Stevie: I got these on a clearance rack at Target.

*Even though they eventually become the best of friends, **David and Stevie** could not be more different in their sense of style.*

As seen on *scarymommy.com,*
January 14, 2021, by Laura Grainger

66

I'm afraid you and I have arrived at an awkward moment in our parent–child relationship … it seems that there are some nude photographs of me on the internet, and I would like you to search for them.

99

Moira enlists David's help
in a rather delicate matter.

As seen on everdaypower.com, November 9, 2020,
by Nia Simone McLeod

"

I don't want to brag, but
Us Weekly once described
me as 'up for anything'.

"

*We're not sure that that's entirely
a good thing, **Alexis.***

As seen on *elitedaily.com, November 4, 2020,
by Rachel Chapman*

"

Yeah, I just feel like the whole
session was rushed. Like,
there was no back lighting,
or emotional direction.

"

*David is not impressed with his experience
getting a driving license.*

As seen on *readersdigest.ca, September 18, 2020,
by Brett Walther*

What is the source of this falsehood? And what photo are they using?

Moira has her priorities in order when rumours of her death circulate on the internet.

As seen on *scarymommy.com, December 22, 2020, by Laura Grainger*

66

I could not be more at one
with nature. I do Coachella
every year.

99

*David's nature-loving credentials
are rather limited.*

As seen on *eonline.com*, April 7, 2020,
by Lauren Piester, Chris Harnick

I want you to know that you are the most important thing in this world to me. You know that, don't you? And I include Caroline in that, and I've had that wig for 40 years. **99**

Moira *assures Johnny that he'll always be her number one, marginally ahead of her favourite wig.*

As seen on *elitedaily.com, January 13, 2020, by Corinne Sullivan*

Oh, look at David. Smart enough to get that joke, but not smart enough to stop wearing sweaters in the middle of summer. **99**

Johnny calls David out
on his signature style.

As seen on *yourtango.com, October 30, 2020,*
by Jaycee Levin

I won't wear anything with an adhesive backing.

Moira *puts her foot down when it comes to name badges.*

As seen on *scarymommy.com, December 22, 2020, by Laura Grainger*

THE FACTS

David Rose is famously unwilling to compromise, but so is Dan Levy. Levy was involved in every aspect of the show, right down to the carpets. Speaking to *GQ*, Levy admitted that he would scuff the carpets himself to make sure they looked suitably run-down. Now that's attention to detail!

These mountaineering shoes that my boyfriend is wearing, looking like Oprah on a Thanksgiving Day hike? Incorrect.

__David__ accidentally calls Patrick his boyfriend for the first time, while insulting his shoes.

As seen on *elitedaily.com, January 13, 2020, by Corinne Sullivan*

66

This isn't *Say Yes to the Dress*, sweetheart. Orange is the new orange.

99

Ronnie *is not falling for any of Alexis's tricks.*

As seen on *elitedaily.com, January 23, 2020, by Marisa Casciano*

Oh, in case you wake up in a chair with your hands duct-taped together, you can snap the duct tape by just raising your hands over your head and then bringing them down really hard.

Alexis *gives some disconcerting advice before a date.*

As seen on elitedaily.com, January 13, 2020, by Corinne Sullivan

> **"** I didn't like the matchy-matchy skirt and blazer. No, she looked like an aging stewardess from a Latvian airline. **"**

***Moira** is not impressed with the style of Schitt's Creek residents.*

As seen on readersdigest.ca, September 18, 2020, by Brett Walther

CHAPTER
FOUR

FOLD IN THE CHEESE

ON FOOD AND FRUIT WINE

Café Tropical is one of Schitt's Creek's busiest and most fashionable eateries, which really isn't saying much. These hilarious quotes with have you spitting out your mystery green smoothies. Yum.

I brought this pie from work,
but on the way, I realized I didn't
check what kind, so there's a 50/50
chance there's meat in it.

Twyla *is always a welcome guest
at any gathering, even if her food
offerings are risky.*

As seen on *elitedaily.com, January 14, 2020,
by Rachel Chapman*

"

There are myriad tactics to boost numbers at your party! Well, you start by comping a few influential guests. You'd be shocked at how many celebrities show up to a thing with the promise of a free Wagyu slider.

"

***Moira** understands the importance of attracting high-class party guests, with fancy food.*

As seen on *readersdigest.ca, September 18, 2020,* by Brett Walther

David: What does that mean? What does 'fold in the cheese' mean?

Moira: You fold it in.

David: I, I understand that, but how, how do you fold it? Do you fold it in half like a piece of paper and drop it in the pot, or what do you do?

Moira: David, I cannot show you everything.

David: OK, well, can you show me one thing?

Moira: You just... here's what you do. You just fold it in.

David: OK, I don't know how to fold broken cheese like that.

FOLD IN THE CHEESE

Moira: David, then I don't know how to be any clearer! You take that thing that's in your hand and you...

David: If you say 'fold in' one more time...

Moira: It says 'fold it in'!

David: This is your recipe! You fold in the cheese then!

Moira: Don't you dare!

David: You fold it in!

Moira: David! Oh good, now I see bubbles. David! What does burning smell like?

"

*The "family" enchilada recipe is a disaster in the hands of **Moira and David.***

As seen on *imdb.com, accessed January 23, 2021*

I heard that someone wants mozzarella sticks for their birthday. I'm pretty sure that I scraped most of the freezer burn off of those.

Twyla's version of fine dining may differ slightly from David's understanding.

As seen on *readersdigest.ca, September 18, 2020,* by Brett Walther

"

We're drinking to me not
becoming an alcoholic.

"

Stevie *finds an appropriate
cause to celebrate.*

As seen on *scarymommy.com, January 14, 2021,
by Laura Grainger*

I Googled that bug. It's some sort of demonic cricket that takes chunks out of your skin when provoked. 'Chunks' is the word that Google used.

David fears that he will become a snack for some unwelcome wildlife.

As seen on *readersdigest.ca, September 18, 2020, by Brett Walther*

66

This wine is awful.
Get me another glass.

99

Moira *acquires a taste for some*
suspect fruit wine.

As seen on *screenrant.com*, March 21, 2020,
by Amanda Steele

> **"** I will not feel shame about the mall pretzels. **"**

David recalls turning to food during a difficult break-up.

As seen on *scarymommy.com, January 14, 2021, by Laura Grainger*

66

I have my own holiday tradition.
It's like the 12 Days of Christmas,
but it's one day with 12 bottles
of wine.

99

*Stevie lays out her plans for
a festive liquid lunch.*

As seen on *yourtango.com, October 30, 2020,*
by Jaycee Levin

> **"**
>
> Well, Jocelyn, there are certain things that are just not done: Smoking in a car with a baby—unless you crack a window; tipping before tax; mixing drinks with cola; and giving away a coat that doesn't belong to you. **"**

__Moira__ abides by a very interesting set of morals.

As seen on *readersdigest.ca*, September 18, 2020, by Brett Walther

THE FACTS

During the filming of season 1, Emily Hampshire, who plays Stevie Budd, mentioned to Dan Levy that Sally Bowles from *Cabaret* was her dream character to play. Well in season 5, Levy made her wish come true! For the final episode of the series, Hampshire, playing Stevie, plays Sally, including a heartfelt rendition of "Maybe This Time". Theatre dreams come true!

##

You smell very flammable right now.

David does his best to look after a very drunk Stevie, perhaps with a fire extinguisher.

As seen on scarymommy.com, January 14, 2021, by Laura Grainger

"

One pizza? What is this,
Les Mis?

"

David *is thoroughly unimpressed*
with Johnny's meal provisions.

As seen on *screenrant.com, August 10, 2019,*
by Amanda Steele

66

Did I used to have a
drinking problem?

99

*Moira does some self-reflection and
ponders the reason she remembers
so little of David and Alexis's childhood.*

As seen on *scarymommy.com, December 22, 2020,
by Laura Grainger*

66

I'm going to need a stiff
drink to get through this.

99

David turns to old coping
mechanisms in trying times.

As seen on *screenrant.com, August 10, 2019,*
by Amanda Steele

A heavy salad might as well
be a casserole.

__Moira__ on healthy eating is always a treat.

As seen on *eonline.com, April 7, 2020,*
by Lauren Piester, Chris Harnick

"

You must prepare for life, and whatever it will throw at you. The opportunities will diminish, and the ass will get bigger. Oh, you can bet your bottom dollar it will! Especially yours. You're going to have a *huge* ass.

"

Moira gives some sincere,
if discomforting, advice.

As seen on everdaypower.com, November 9, 2020,
by Nia Simone McLeod

THE FACTS

Annie Murphy didn't just skate through her role as spoiled socialite Alexis. From the way she held her bag to the way she talked, Murphy channelled some of Hollywood's infamous it-girls. She spent hours watching YouTube clips of the Kardashians, Lindsay Lohan, the Olsen twins and Paris Hilton to find her unique voice. Like, literally.

I ordered the one with the highest alcohol content.

Roland *starts off the party the right way.*

As seen on *elitedaily.com, January 6, 2020,*
by Rachel Chapman

Welcome. Hope you're enjoying the cinnamon buns and vodka. We thought it was festive in a Scandinavian sort of way.

Johnny tries to give the motel's impromptu happy hour an international feel.

As seen on *eonline.com*, April 7, 2020, by Lauren Piester, Chris Harnick

66

If that's not a cause for alcohol,
I don't know what is!

99

*According to **Moira**,
it's always wine o'clock.*

As seen on scarymommy.com, December 22, 2020,
by Laura Grainger

CHAPTER
FIVE

LEO IN BALI

SHOWBIZ AND CELEBRITY

There's no doubt that the Rose family was well connected, once. From Alexis's jet-setting stories to Moira's tenure as a soap opera star, show business and celebrity had followed the Rose family from Bali to Bosnia. Or, in other words, from the A-list to Schitt list.

I've always wanted to be slapped by Vivien Blake.

*TMI there, **Roland.***

As seen on *elitedaily.com, January 6, 2021,*
by Rachel Chapman

66

Your wayfaring thespian
has returned.

99

Moira announces her return
from an on-location shoot.

As seen on *scarymommy.com, December 22, 2020,*
by Laura Grainger

66

Oh, that is my favourite
Liam Neeson movie.

99

Twyla *on a movie that does*
not have Liam Neeson in it.

As seen on *elitedaily.com, January 14, 2020,*
by Rachel Chapman

"

The last time I felt this emotionally encumbered, I was playing Lady Macbeth on a Crystal Skies cruise ship during Shakespeare at Sea Week.

"

Moira resonates a bit too well with a murderous Shakespearean character.

As seen on *scarymommy.com*, December 22, 2020, by Laura Grainger

66

Mutt: Okay, what would we have talked about? It's my face.

Alexis: Um, you'd have said, uh, 'Wow, Alexis, I'm thinking about shaving my beard.' And then I would've said, 'Hmm. No, Mutt, I don't think that that's the right journey for you at this point in time.'

Mutt: Well, then I would've said, 'Too bad.' I shave like, every six months. Okay, you try growing a beard!

Alexis: I was a beard for a very well-known actor, and I get it, it's uncomfortable.

Alexis *has a very…ah… interesting take on facial hair.*

As seen on *tvquot.es, accessed January 23, 2020*

66

Alexis: What's your favourite season?
Moira: Awards.

99

Alexis and Moira *share some bonding time.*

As seen on *eonline.com, April 7, 2020,*
by Lauren Piester, Chris Harnick

I know all about being left in the lurch for a fundraiser. Eva Longoria and I were supposed to perform our ventriloquist act for the Everybody Nose benefit for juvenile rhinoplasty, when she suddenly drops out due to exhaustion. I had to be both puppet and puppeteer.

Moira sympathizes with Jocelyn on the difficulties of event management.

As seen on *readersdigest.ca, September 18, 2020, by Brett Walther*

EW, DAVID!

I was casually seeing Prince Harry, so there was the whole, like, 'Is she gonna be a princess' thing… um, but it's also because we were going through this very dark phase where we were just, like, partying too hard.

Alexis *on the time when she nearly went from Hollywood princess to real royalty.*

As seen on scarymommy.com, January 14, 2021, by Laura Grainger

> **"**
> Politics 101, John. When you have limited resources, your best course of action is to create a stir. It's exciting. It's fun. It's like that episode of *Sunrise Bay* when I stole my own bébé. **"**

Moira takes her acting experience into her campaign for town council.

As seen on *readersdigest.ca, September 18, 2020,* by Brett Walther

My name is Alexis, and yes, I did not finish high school. Um, it's this long, boring story involving a yacht, and a famous soccer player, and like a *ton* of mushrooms. 99

*As high school dropout stories go, **Alexis's** is pretty compelling.*

As seen on *scarymommy.com, January 14, 2021, by Laura Grainger*

❝

The live crows on set welcomed me as one of their own. One even tried to mate. **❞**

Moira gives a prime example of why one should never work with animals or children.

As seen on *everdaypower.com, November 9, 2020,* by Nia Simone McLeod

THE FACTS

Not only is *Schitt's Creek* a fan favourite, but it won a record-breaking nine awards at the 2020 Emmys, including categories in all four best actor categories, writing, costumes, casting, directing, editing, hair and make-up. This sweep beat the previous record of five awards in one night, held by *The Marvellous Mrs. Maisel* since 2018.

66

What now? Do I leave everything behind and move to some random island to be with the love of my life? Because I did that with Harry Styles in England, and it was, like, too rainy.

99

*When deciding whether or not to follow Ted to the Galápagos Islands, **Alexis** has some previous experience to fall back on.*

As seen on *elitedaily.com*, November 4, 2020, by Rachel Chapman

66

When one of us shines,
all of us shine.

99

*__Moira__ educating the Jazzagals on
the true meaning of "ensemble".*

As seen on everdaypower.com, November 9, 2020,
by Nia Simone McLeod

66

I went on a blind date to
Bali with Leo, so I'm pretty
sure it'll be fine.

99

Dating in Schitt's Creek is no challenge to
Alexis *after her international experiences.*

As seen on *scarymommy.com, January 14, 2021,*
by Laura Grainger

Oh, I won't wait for anyone's decision. I once got Winnie Mandela to RSVP to an Artists Against Eczema benefit within the hour.

Moira's powers of persuasion were honed in rather high-stakes scenarios.

As seen on readersdigest.ca, September 18, 2020, by Brett Walther

Yeah, no. I know composting. Gwyneth Paltrow does a compost gift exchange.

*At least **Alexis's** star-studded life came with a side helping of eco-consciousness.*

As seen on scarymommy.com, January 14, 2021, by Laura Grainger

Is 'tests' code for open heart surgery? You can tell me, I once played a nurse on *M.A.S.H.*

*Is someone going to tell **Moira** that film medicine isn't real?*

As seen on *readersdigest.ca*, September 18, 2020, by *Brett Walther*

"

I used to text Zac Efron just, like, for a booty call. Poor thing would be pressing the buzzer before I even hit send.

"

*Who knew the High School Musical heartthrob was one of **Alexis's** former admirers?*

As seen on *elitedaily.com, November 4, 2020, by Rachel Chapman*

66

You just watch a season
of *Girls* and do the opposite
of what they do.

99

David's *advice for thriving in*
New York City seems straightforward.

As seen on *scarymommy.com, January 14, 2021,*
by Laura Grainger

THE FACTS

Did you watch *Schitt's Creek* and feel that Moira, played by Catherine O'Hara, looked familiar? You're not the only one! Seasonal viewers of *Schitt's Creek* often discover that O'Hara plays a central role in the Christmas holiday favourite *Home Alone* as Kevin McCallister's frantic mum. For the spooky lovers, she also plays Delia Deetz (Winona Ryder's mum) in the Halloween classic *Beetlejuice*. Kevin … I mean, David!

Fear not, she hath risen!

Moira *announces her resurrection*
in a typically dramatic fashion.

As seen on *eonline.com, April 7, 2020,*
by Lauren Piester, Chris Harnick

> I worked in soaps. They had me play my own father, who then became pregnant despite the vasectomy. I still hold the record for the longest-running demonic possession on daytime television.

Moira *on the twists and turns of daytime television soap operas.*

As seen on *readersdigest.ca*, September 18, 2020
by Brett Walther

Hello, my name is Alexis Rose represented by Alexis Rose Talent. I have chosen to perform the title track off of my critically reviewed, limited reality series, *A Little Bit Alexis*. Feel free to sing along if you know the words!

I'm a Lamborghini
I'm a Hollywood star
I'm a little bit tipsy
When I drive my car

I'm expensive sushi
I'm a cute huge yacht
I'm a little bit single
Even when I'm not
I'm a little bit, I'm a little bit,
I'm a little bit, I'm a little bit,
La la la la la la la
A little bit Alexis

"

As seen on *eonline.com, April 7, 2020,*
by Lauren Piester, Chris Harnick

CHAPTER
SIX

BÉBÉ

FAMILY AFFAIRS

The Rose family, despite their riches-to-rags downfall, are a family just like any other. They bicker, they laugh, they make each other's lives 100 times harder, but at the end of the day they love each other very much. Love that journey for us.

> Are we terrible parents?

*The answer is yes, **Moria**,
but don't worry, you'll make up for it.*

As seen on scarymommy.com, December 22, 2020,
by Laura Grainger

What kind of sociopath abandons her family in some vomit-soaked dump to gallivant around the world with her dumb, shipping-heir, loser boyfriend she's known for three months?!

David is thoroughly unimpressed with Alexis's plans to jet off with Stavros.

As seen on mamasgeeky.com, January 7, 2020, by Mama's Geeky

There once was a radiant young actress who dreamed of having two sons.

__Moira__ tells her only daughter, Alexis, a comforting bedtime story.

As seen on scarymommy.com, December 22, 2020, by Laura Grainger

66

Fall off a bridge, please.

99

David to Alexis during one of
their many fights. Lovely.

As seen on mamasgeeky.com, January 7, 2020,
by Mama's Geeky

Johnny: Moira, have you seen the kids?

Moira: Whose kids?

Moira isn't exactly on the same page as her husband.

As seen on *scarymommy.com, December 22, 2020, by Laura Grainger*

"

If airplane safety videos have taught me anything, David, it's that a mother puts her own mask on first.

"

Moira's *approach to parenting is rather intriguing.*

As seen on yourtango.com, October 30, 2020, by Jaycee Levin

No matter what anyone says,
you will always be our first dad.

David *to Johnny on the news
that Moira may run off with Roland.*

As seen on *scarymommy.com, January 14, 2021,
by Laura Grainger*

"

You'd think there'd be more of a market for oversized paintings of other people's families. **"**

Stevie identifies a niche gap in the market.

As seen on yourtango.com, October 30, 2020, by Jaycee Levin

"

Moira: We all have to go,
   David, unless you have some
   special excuse.
David: It's my birthday.

"

Alexis's graduation is turned into
a family affair, against David's will.

As seen on scarymommy.com, December 22, 2020,
by Laura Grainger

"

You strike me as the sort
of person that had a hard
time in high school.

"

Jocelyn *accurately and painfully summarizes*
David's educational experience.

As seen on *yourtango.com, October 30, 2020,*
by Jaycee Levin

"

Moira: Who put a picture
of a ghost on my desk?
Roland: …That's the sonogram
of our baby!

"

Moira misidentifies a
very important envelope.

As seen on *scarymommy.com, December 22, 2020,*
by Laura Grainger

THE FACTS

Eugene Levy and Catherine O'Hara are not only married in the TV show, the pair go back a long time in real life as well! They both started as young actors together in the improvisational theatre troupe The Second City and remained firm friends since then. Other notable entertainers that got their start in The Second City include Bill Murray, Mike Myers, Steve Carell, Tina Fey and Amy Poehler!

> **"**
> Just think of them as tiny little roommates whose tiny little poops you get to clean up. **"**

Alexis *on the joys of motherhood,*
a joy that David does not share.

As seen on *scarymommy.com, January 14, 2021,*
by Laura Grainger

"

I'd really like you to sing at my cousin's funeral. She's not dead, but she's been coughing a lot lately.

"

Roland is planning ahead for some unfortunate extended family members.

As seen on scarymommy.com, January 14, 2021, by Laura Grainger

66

You do realize the bébé
is crying?

99

Moira and Johnny *play babysitter, and*
instantly find it challenging without a nanny.

As seen on scarymommy.com, December 22, 2020,
by Laura Grainger

66

John, how was I to know you were in peril? You keep everything inside, like a bashful clam!

Moira *on the importance of communication in marriage.*

As seen on *readersdigest.ca, September 18, 2020, by Brett Walther*

99

Moira: I will not relive that
bullying nightmare.
David: Uh, it wasn't that bad.
Moira: That's the heart-breaking
part. You were so blissfully
unaware.

*__Moira__ waring Alexis not to be a
pushover, unlike her older brother.*

As seen on *scarymommy.com, December 22, 2020,
by Laura Grainger*

"

Stop doing that with your face. **"**

Alexis to David, or rather David's face, which
needs to stop doing that thing, immediately.

As seen on *elitedaily.com*, November 4, 2020,
by Rachel Chapman

66

Moira: I've been calling David and he's not picking up!
Johnny: And what about Alexis?
Moira: There's an idea… Anybody have her number?

99

*In a family emergency, **Moira** can always be called upon to forget her children's phone numbers.*

As seen on *scarymommy.com, December 22, 2020, by Laura Grainger*

THE FACTS

Schitt's Creek is a thoroughly family affair. Not only did father–son duo Eugene and Dan Levy write and direct the show, but sister Sarah Levy plays waitress Twyla. As children, the siblings were always putting on shows for family members and wrote and acted in high school productions. Eventually, Sarah studied theatre and Dan went to film school. The talent must be genetic!

66

What you did was impulsive, capricious, and melodramatic. But, it was also wrong.

99

__Moira__ scolding David, despite being slightly proud of his inherited capatciy for the melodramatic.

As seen on screenrant.com, March 21, 2020, by Amanda Steele

"

Moira: You're the ill one, but I'm feeling this…

Alexis: Maternal instinct, maybe?

Moira: No, that's not it.

"

*Bedside manners aren't exactly one of **Moira's** strong suits.*

As seen on scarymommy.com, December 22, 2020, by Laura Grainger

Where is bébé's chamber?

Moira *acquaints herself with*
Roland Schitt Jnr's sleeping quarters.

As seen on *buzzfeed.com, September 27, 2020,*
by Josie Ayre, Sam Ciel

Alexis…something Rose.

Another outstanding parental moment from **Moira** *as she forgets Alexis's middle name.*

As seen on scarymommy.com, December 22, 2020,
by Laura Grainger

CHAPTER
SEVEN

YOU'RE SIMPLY THE BEST

AWWH-INSPIRING LOVE QUOTES

You're simply the best! Love is all around in *Schitt's Creek*, whether it's 30 years of marriage, make-ups or break-ups, the Rose family have been through it all. The heart wants what the heart wants, no matter what the label or the bottle.

EW, DAVID!

Umm, I do drink red wine, but I also drink white wine… And I've been known to sample the occasional rosé. And a couple summers back, I tried a merlot that used to be a chardonnay, which got a bit complicated. I like the wine, not the label.

David *on versatility in romance.*

As seen on readersdigest.ca, September 18, 2020, by Brett Walther

I have to say, I think that you are
the most beautiful girl this town's
ever seen.

Ted *is completely smitten over Alexis.*

As seen on *elitedaily.com, January 13, 2020,
by Corinne Sullivan*

He loves everyone. Men, women, women who become men, men who become women. I'm his father, and I always wanted his life to be easy. But, you know, just pick one gender, and maybe, maybe everything would've been less confusing.

Johnny expresses bewilderment over David's romantic choices.

As seen on *scarymommy.com, January 14, 2021, by Laura Grainger*

"

I'm starting to feel like I'm trapped in an Avril Lavigne lyric here. **"**

David and Stevie find themselves in a rather complicated romantic situation.

As seen on *readersdigest.ca, September 18, 2020,*
by Brett Walther

66

He hasn't even asked for my phone number, which in my experience means he's either newly married or he's gay.

99

Alexis gets snubbed by Patrick, and suspects that David might have something to do with it.

As seen on *readersdigest.ca, September 18, 2020, by Brett Walther*

66

It's rare to find someone this beautiful, and smart, and deeply selfish, yet charming.

99

Ted *on all the things that he loves about Alexis. Cute.*

As seen on *elitedaily.com, January 13, 2020, by Corinne Sullivan*

Roland: Well, you know, Johnny, when it comes to matters of the heart, we can't tell our kids who to love. Who said that?
Johnny: You did.

Johnny and Roland discuss watching their children struggle with dating.

As seen on *scarymommy.com, January 14, 2021,* by Laura Grainger

66

David, you have to stop watching *Notting Hill*. It's not helpful for our relationship.

99

Patrick *tries to limit David's romantic expectations.*

As seen on *readersdigest.ca, September 18, 2020, by Brett Walther*

You're like a poem. Like, a really pretty poem… or like, a mermaid, or something.

Alexis *has a way with words when it comes to expressing her feelings toward Ted.*

As seen on *elitedaily.com, January 13, 2020, by Corinne Sullivan*

THE FACTS

Dan Levy has been vocal about the importance of David as an LGBTQ+ character. Levy wanted to ensure the character could just be, as opposed to their sexuality becoming part of the storyline. David is pansexual, and while his orientation is treated with humour, Levy chose not to give him a coming–out moment, as he told *GQ*, "It's not a cross that straight people have to bear."

66

He told me he doesn't want
my help, so I'm just going to
play the supportive partner
and watch him fail.

99

*David's take on healthy relationship
dynamics is really something.*

As seen on scarymommy.com, January 14, 2021,
by Laura Grainger

66

Best–case scenario, you realize
how good you have it with me.
Worst–case scenario, you realize
how good you have it with me.

99

David spots a win-win scenario
in his relationship with Patrick.

As seen on *elitedaily.com, January 13, 2020,*
by Corinne Sullivan

❝

I've never liked a smile as much
as I like yours.

❞

*David gets honest, and
very sweet, with Patrick.*

As seen on *elitedaily.com, January 13, 2020,
by Corinne Sullivan*

66

Do I wear my fringed vest?
Or, more importantly, do
I wear anything under it?

99

Patrick *prepares for date night.*

As seen on *scarymommy.com, January 14, 2021,*
by Laura Grainger

So this is weird. Today marks the longest relationship I've ever voluntarily had with someone. Yeah, the actual longest relationship was a three-month affair with a Saudi prince, but for the last two months of that I was trapped in his palace trying to get to an embassy.

Alexis *marks her three-month anniversary with Ted by recalling a relationship that wasn't as great.*

As seen on *elitedaily.com, January 13, 2020, by Corinne Sullivan*

66

As if I didn't see this coming.
He's broken up with me five times
already. Like there was that time
that he never met me in Rio. And
remember that time when he gave
me his ex-wife's engagement ring?
And then there was that time last
summer when he left his molly in
my glove compartment and then
I got arrested.

99

Alexis on her break-up with Stravos that
she definitely did not see coming.

As seen on scarymommy.com, January 14, 2021,
by Laura Grainger

"

Beep, beep! Paging Dr. Casanova J. Heartbreaker!

"

Alexis and Ted *do a spot of role-playing.*

As seen on *elitedaily.com, January 13, 2020,*
by Corinne Sullivan

66

You're simply the best.

99

Patrick *is impressed as David channels his inner Tina Turner.*

As seen on *elitedaily.com, January 13, 2020,* by Corinne Sullivan

THE FACTS

David and Patrick's relationship not only inspired countless "awwhs"; it also moved viewers to contact Dan Levy with their own stories. Fans continue to reach out to Levy on social media and even stop him in the street to thank him for his portrayal of the relationship, telling him how it has impacted their lives and relationships with conservative family members. Speaking to *GQ*, Levy recalled how a mother wrote to Levy to thank him for easing her fears around her son coming out. When Levy first got the message, it reduced him to tears. "She's been able to feel like he's going to be okay," he said, "because these characters are okay."

"

My little Galapa-guy!

"

Alexis on Ted's new-found island life.

As seen on *elitedaily.com, January 13, 2020,*
by Corinne Sullivan

You're my Mariah Carey.

Patrick *on why David is his favourite diva.*

As seen on *mamasgeeky.com. January 7, 2020,
by Mama's Geeky*

Um, yes, love this journey for us.

*We love that journey
for you too, **Alexis**.*

As seen on *elitedaily.com, January 13, 2020,
by Corinne Sullivan*

66

You are my happy ending.

99

David on happily ever afters.

As seen on *elitedaily.com, January 13, 2020,*
by Corinne Sullivan